The riv...
which connect us
to the past

The rivers which connect us to the past

PETER HORN

Mayibuye History and Literature Series No. 68

MAYIBUYE
BOOKS—UWC

Published 1996 in southern Africa by
Mayibuye Books, University of the Western Cape, Private
Bag X17, Bellville 7535, South Africa

Mayibuye Books is the book publishing division of the
Mayibuye Centre at the University of the Western Cape. The
Mayibuye Centre is a pioneering project helping to recover
areas of South African history that have been neglected in
the past. It also provides space for cultural creativity and
expression in a way that promotes the process of change and
reconstruction in a democratic South Africa. The Mayibuye
History and Literature Series is part of this project. The
series editors are Barry Feinberg and André Odendaal.

ISBN 1-86808-303-9

By the same author:
Poems:
Voices from the Gallows Trees (Ophir 1969)
Walking through our Sleep (Ravan 1974)
Silence in Jail (Scribe 1978)
Civil War Cantos (Scribe 1987)
Poems 1964–1989 (Ravan 1991)
An Axe in the Ice (COSAW 1992)
Derrière le vernis du soleil, poèmes 1964–1989 (europePoésie 1993)

Anthology:
Kap der Guten Hoffnung. Gedichte aus dem Südafrikanischen Widerstand
(Athenäum 1980)

Short stories:
The Kaffir who reads Books (COSAW, forthcoming: 1996)

Essays:
Heinrich von Kleists Erzählungen. Eine Einführung (1978)
Kleist-Chronik (1980)
Writing my Reading. Essays on Literary Politics in South Africa
(Amsterdam/Atlanta: Rodopi 1994)

**With financial assistance from the Royal Netherlands Embassy
and the Swedish International Development Cooperation Agency
(SIDA)**

PRINTED AND BOUND IN THE REPUBLIC OF SOUTH AFRICA
BY THE RUSTICA PRESS (PTY) LTD, NDABENI, WESTERN CAPE
D5158

Contents

The 'free spirit' has to find its sensuality again. It has to make sure of its own liveliness. Only in this way can it become 'aesthetic'. Although art as a potency of the 'free spirit' is necessarily intellectual and individual, it nevertheless draws its very own power from this sensuality. In it it finds its elementary meaning. Going back to the 'meaning of the earth' all creativity has a cosmic, a geological and a biological dimension.

Gerhardt, Volker 1992, *Friedrich Nietzsche* München: Beck. 205

The rivers which connect us to the past

Long before there was Africa

principio terram, ne non aequalis ab omni
parte foret, magni speciem glomeravit in orbis
at first he formed the earth, so it did not lack symmetry
in all parts, into an enormous sphere.
      Publius Ovidius Naso, *Metamorphoses*, Liber 1:34-35

1

No sun lit up the universe
with its spectrum of sparkling colours
and no moon grew fat
under its grazing horns every month
and no milky way graced the ether
as the highway of the Gods
and there was no earth, no ocean, no air
no gods walked large in the dreams of humans
and no humans crawled on this planet
to dream of gods, and there was no love
in this vast nothingness of whirling
subatomic particles.

The non-not-being:
there never was a beginning
out of nothing.
Until in a billionth of a second
the unforeseen happened
the loudest ever bang, when matter
raced faster than light
through micro-millimetres of space,
but with no ears to hear it
and no air to transmit it.

Because we, the sun, the earth,
the whirl of the milky way

we *are* the bang: we *are* the wave
travelling with nearly the speed of light
to the unknown curved unendingness
of the universe.

In the whirling dust
unseen by any eye
the sun formed and flamed
with its hydrogen oven
and the earth
particles falling into the glowing pressure
of an enormous mass
began to flow and emit light.

Enormous the light
of the flaming sky
hanging weightlessly
above the crust of the earth
which was swimming on hot and molten magma
in whirls which blew up lava fountains
and engulfed the broken shards
of the continents arising out of the turbulence
of creation.

And far into the dark space the light air
filled with water vapour and sulphur dioxide
sparkled in the neon light of gigantic
                                    thunderstorms
lashing the earth.
And it was there
in a pool filled with slimy proteins
built from coal and water
that life was sparked by millions of volts.

Long before gods existed
fragments of crust were squeezed

in the turmoil and sand washed
into a primeval sea swarming with algae
and bacteria somewhere near Barberton
three billion and eight hundred million
years ago: green cells which fabricated
starches out of sunlight and carbon dioxide
and the wonder of life began.

2

Nobody can remember the path
of the continents across the planet
and the bursts of magma, the earthquakes
which shifted these huge blocks of rock
from one place to another:
only the wounds and sutures
the remnants of giant mountains
from the Richtersveld to Natal
and the thousands of feet of sand
washed into the sea and compacted into sandstone
towering more than a thousand meter
above Cape Town
after millions of years
tell us of the unthinkable forces
which shaped this continent
long before there were men and women
and long before a god looked out
from the mirror of millions of souls
through the eyes of humans
and found that everything was good.

3

Nobody remembers the names and the sources
of rivers that washed the gold

into the Witwatersrand Basin,
nobody ever heard the original name
of the Gondwana continent
which stretched from New Zealand to Chile.
The wind has forgotten it
and the lava flows in the Drakensberg
bear no inscription.

Long before there was any God
who could map out the six day work week
and create the names of the animals and plants
to inscribe them in holy books
the dinosaurs walked through the swampy Karoo
and the glossopteris trees unfolded their leathery
                                        leaves.

But life was never lost
however many died: algae and
swordfish and shark
and the slowly creeping snails
whose trails are preserved in the sandstone
all had their day in the light of the sun
and the sun was glorious.

Red blood flowed from the wounds
of primitive fishes and frogs
bones were broken by the giant jaws of Tyrannus
                                        Rex
stomachs contracted in hunger and drought
but life itself survived for three billion years
an unlikely but courageous film
on the rocky surface of the earth and the giant
                                        ocean.

4

No one was there when the great volcano erupted
near Walvis Bay one hundred twenty million years
                                             ago
and tore the continent apart
shifting South America thousands of kilometres to
the West.
No one was there when the Falkland Islands
said good bye to the coast of Durban
when Antarctica and Australia went on a journey
to the South and the East
and through the rent poured millions of cubic meter
of molten lava onto the Mountains of Spears
over millions of years.
No one was there when India prepared to meet Asia,
no mind, no human or god, when the Himalayas
rose out of the Indian Ocean
to celebrate that wedding.
No one was there when the Alps
were formed out of the slime of the abyss.

The daughters of Lot

quem dixere Chaos: rudis indigestaque moles,
nec quicquam nisi pondus iners congestaque eodem
non bene iunctarum discordia semina rerum.
which was called Chaos: a rough, formless mass
nothing but sluggish weight and, discordant,
the germs of matter, heaped on each other in
a confused jumble
Publius Ovidius Naso, *Metamorphoses*, Liber 1:7-9

1

Goethe, facing the threat of the French Revolution
this gigantic social upheaval,
saw it in the image of a volcano, and
was looking for some immovable *Urgestein,*
some unshakeable granite underneath
the shifting appearances: some being, a *Ding an sich*
on which to build the house of his life.

We need this: the belief
that at least the rocks under our feet
are stable and that there is a God
from before time until after time
that there is a sameness and a saneness
and a pattern: even the laws of nature
satisfy our hunger for stability
and ward off our fear of change
which is a fear of death.

We deny that the earth moves
around the sun in our language
which says the sun is rising
even if we know that the earth is turning
and language tells us this is rock-certain

and unshakeable while the earthquake
heaves and shears at the familiar features
of the landscape, its very rock bottom unstable
and granite is nothing but the frozen magma
of ancient volcanoes.

We talk about human nature
as if we had never heard about evolution and
                                        history:
we talk about the eternal harmony of the heavens
when even children learn that the orderly
                                        symphony
of God is the loud crash of an explosion
and the chaotic whirl of substances
through uncharted regions of a disorderly universe.

2

Zeus is always victorious in the myths of the rulers:
even the giants who build towering mountains
to reach the sky and to topple the tyrant
are lying in their blood which covers the plains of
                                        the earth
to testify against the possibility of change.

But born of their blood emerged human beings
who detested the Gods: revolutionaries
who set out to change the world.
And all the conferences of the mighty
will not wipe them off the earth.

But like Zeus they always use propaganda
to smear their opponents: barbarians they are,
they cook and fry their prisoners of war,
cannibals and wild animals who drink the blood of
                                        cows

and they take away their voice with which they
                                    could prove
their humanity in speech.

3

Nothing is too much for the rulers
who fancy themselves descendants of Gods
which they created to fill the void in the hierarchy:
nothing: when Zeus unleashed his royal anger
over the descendants of the rebels
he burned the earth with lightning until the Gods
were afraid that the ether itself would perish
in this conflagration and the axis of the earth,
and land and sea, and the palace of the mighty.

When the generals threatened with nuclear bombs
they forgot about the earth and the water and the
                                    plants
and the enormous radiating desert in their rage
to destroy the enemy: whose thoughts - no their
                                    practice -
threatened the exploitation of ever more rebellious
                                    workers.
Safely in their bunkers they prepared the end of the
                                    world
the super lightning flash which would cook all
                                    human beings
alive: the ultimate barbarians and cannibals.

8

4

We talk about human nature, as if what we call
                                    human
had not been that which is not nature: our poems
as well as our bombs. The unpredictable thought
which links some cells in the brain
to other cells where there never was a pathway
                                    before.

To be human is to produce the unlawful,
that which the tyrannous gods have always
                                    punished,
the skyscrapers of Babylon and the sins of Sodom.

To be human means to be drowned in the Flood
and to be burned to ashes
to be human means to be made into salt pillars
when you enrage the tyrant
and to be nailed to the rock like Prometheus
with an obedient imperial bird hacking open your
                                    belly.

But when they escape from sulphur and brimstone
and when the mother has turned into salt
the daughters of Lot commit incest again
little concerned about eternal unnatural laws.

Kissing the cold stone

atque ita "si precibus" dixerunt "numina iustis
victa remollescunt, si flectitur ira deorum"
and they spoke: "let us see, if the anger of the gods
can be softened by just prayer"
    Publius Ovidius Naso, *Metamorphoses* Liber 1:377-
    378

1

In the beginning there were no gods.
There was nature which was that all embracing
continuum of sky and clouds and rain and drought
and sand and sea and plants and animals
in which they found themselves not the strongest.

In the beginning there was a light behind the eye
and a voice between the ears
which spoke in the calm of the noon
when the sun of Africa burned down on them
and in the shade.

In the beginning there was fear in the killing
of horses and zebras and antelopes,
the fear of those who had no carnassials
like the lion or the wild dog or the leopard or the
                             cheetah.
In the beginning there was fear in the killing
of these unaccustomed predators
roaming the steppes of Africa
and the slopes of the valley where Africa is tearing
                             apart
marvelling at the flaming gashes and the boiling
                             lakes
and the ice-capped volcanoes.

In the beginning there was fear and the search
for a firm rock on which to stand in the shifting of
plates.
In the beginning there was a voice which said:
Sister and Woman.
Brother and Man.
In the beginning there were no names
for father and mother or sister and brother or son
and daughter.

2

In the beginning there were no words
but the first word uttered engendered the second:
as no word has any meaning on its own
the first word implied all the others
which had yet to be invented.

The thoughts which were thought in the caves
have disappeared with the brains
out of the skulls which we dig out
at Sterkfontein and Makapansgat.
Yet these thoughts in the light of the fire
implied all possible thoughts
which could be thought by a human brain.

In the beginning there were no poets
but the first poem crafted engendered the second:
as no poem has any meaning on its own
the first poem implied all the others
which had yet to be written
and all poems written remember the first.

In the beginning there were no painters
but the first scratch in a cave's wall led to another:
the hands painted in outline

11

led to a picture of an elephant and that
to the image of an antelope
to the dancing around the fire and the drums
preserved on ancient rock.

3

In the beginning language traced borders
between adjacent thoughts
but it was still easy to cross these borders
and to find new seams between thoughts.

Sounds signal the frontiers between meanings
but the meanings are unstable
and father was not always a father
and family neither a family which we know
and who is your sister is not a biological fact
but a decision of a shaman.

Your ancestor is not the flesh rotting in the earth
nor the bones exhumed by the scientist:
your ancestor is the law of the ancients
hidden in the words of your changeable language
the gestures of love between men and women
and the blood which spills in the kraal
to reaffirm the bond of the people
with their past which is present.

4

Eshu threw a stone yesterday.
He killed a bird today.
Legba uttered a word thousands of years ago.
He finds you obedient today.
Because Legba is the master of language.

His rhythms are the foundations of our world.

The revelation of ourselves as
Fa, the destiny of each individual,
is revealed to us when we tie words
to our reproductive urges: and are called
man or woman

Language discloses the inner shapes
of every human who speaks and his village
and the patterns of time to come
the true form of the world itself.
When you kiss the cold stone of the altar
you kiss the trace of the past
and the words which gave this altar meaning.

5

In the beginning
the Gods were words to describe the world.

Because each person is a bundle of forces
which has nothing to do with himself:
even his *destiny* is inscribed in a language,
his most characteristic wave of the hand
a choice from a repertoire.
The *soul* was handed on from ancestor to ancestor
and each living being was merely
the representative of that indescribable being
which never ceased, because it was life.
The *shadow* which followed a person around
as he or she made her way across the grass of the
                                        steppe
and which disappeared in the shadows of trees
was the indestructible essence of the person
which leaves the body when the bones are buried

and inhabits the night forever.
The *quality*, mobile, and sentient, life,
the power which brings riches or poverty,
the ability to be happy or despondent
draws on a limited vocabulary.

In the beginning
the Gods were words to describe the world.

The rivers which connect us to the past

spumosis volvitur undis,
deiectuque gravi tenues agitantia fumos
nubila conducit, summisque adspergine silvis
impluit et sonitu plus quam vicina fatigat.
it heaves its foaming waves
and gathers above the heavy falls of water clouds of
dust

which send forth delicate veils further away and spray
the peaks of the rising forest, and it stuns with its roar
more than the immediate neighbourhood
  Publius Ovidius Naso, *Metamorphoses*, Liber 1:
570--573

1

This primordial founder: where are his and her
bones buried?

Forgotten, except in myths whose meaning has been
lost.

But the rivers have been flowing
as long as there were humans
who followed them into the mountains of Abyssinia
through tropical forest and through deserts
like arteries of life
From Lake Victoria through the Swamps of the
Sudd

the humidity and the thickets, the nameless
thunder,

the steppes and the Sahara Desert.

In the upper regions of the Blue Nile
amongst the Amhara in the Choke Mountains
in the gravel and sand, perhaps,
the oldest human, the ancestor of us all,

15

roasting his meat over fire,
long before black and white,
long before European, African, Asian,
long before race or colour:
far beyond the reach of our memory.

Migrating down to the limits of the continent,
along the big lakes of Tanzania and Malawi
across the Zambezi and its thundering waterfall
across the droughtstricken Limpopo
amid the flamebush they walked
and in the darkness of the ironwood
and the light was shadowy and mild
and over the glaring grass fields of the High Veld
the yellowish Vaal and the dirty Orange
the rocky Karoo and the steep passes
staring into the open sea from Cape Point
where the earth ends and giant whales
give birth to their milk-sucking fry
and the gulls and cormorants screech
over the sudden rocks plunging into the turmoil.

While at the same time crossing the Sahara
not yet a desert, following the Nile,
the narrow bridge across the Suez
into the fertile crescent
spreading to Europe and Asia
and even into the unknown Americas
humanity conquered the earth.

The life of hunters who braved the buffel and the
eland,
who even dared the lion who threatened their kill
who caught elephants in clever traps and hunted
the fleet zebras over cliffs to their collective death.

16

The life of herders: nothing has been lost,
the admiration of the speckle-backed bull
the pride of the herd and the hundred names
of the many forms of cows
and the roundness of the kraal
where the ancestors come to drink with the living.

2

The river which runs through us like the mighty
                              Congo
is our destiny, and the rock which is hurled
and crushes a skull is not separate from the failure
of courage which caught up with you in that
                              moment
when matter and matter collide to terminate your
                              life.

The firebush has roots which penetrate granite
and cling to the vertical rock: there are fish
which swim in boiling water, and the penguin's
                              chicks
are warmed only by the warmth of the feet of their
                              parents
against the ice of the glaciers which are their nests.

The rock follows lines of the spirit and lines of your
                              genes:

biology and ethics interact, the torn and squashed
                              brain
records your aggression, your tolerance.
You haven't consulted the lines of force which
                              determine your fate.
You have stepped off the wrong bus. You have
                              chosen

the wrong political party. Mistakes are deadly.

Man is not a slave: but his life is bound to the world,
attempts to live in a dream end in disaster.
When all is well, destiny remains hidden, but faults
and cracks tell you that the basement is sagging
and the hole to swallow your house is waiting
for the final shift of the rock layers to swallow it all.

The river which runs through us like the endless
                                        Nile
is our destiny, and the spear which penetrates our
                                        breast
is not separate from the fate in our heart.

3

Divination is the alphabet of our destiny, plain and
                                        open
for all to be seen but seen by few: because of our
                                        fears.
It does not help to throw the bones of the monkey
or to dissect the liver of the pig:
Before your very eyes lies life's openness: always.
We are before our destiny and we modify it
by thinking or by stupidity, by our dreams.
The future is always entailed in our present gestures
and the harvest of our past will starve us blindly.
The meat which we did not eat will shrink our brain
and the poison in the rivers will poison our nerves
the future is entailed in this action now:
the missing schoolbook spells lower wages in ten
                                        years.
Our destiny was written into our history ten
                        thousand years ago

and yesterday again: the murderer with his
$$\text{shotgun.}$$

4

It is of little avail if we hammer our foreheads
against a stone or to torture our hearts with sharp
$$\text{needles}$$
and to fill our stomachs with bitter water.
Forgetting feeds our life like rotting leaves
on the floor of a forest in the rain:
The darkness which hides our imminent death
allows us to climb the buttress. Stupidity fuels the
$$\text{motion}$$
towards a tragic end: knowing
freezes our motion towards a goal
which we will never reach.

The poem is an awful thing
it announces destiny:
the poet is enjoined to name the pain
which he would like to be soothed and eliminated:
he is destined to live between the burning houses
and the hacked off limbs, the children killed
to serve a will to power which never regards life
as anything but an obstacle which must be crushed.

Solitary figures in the palaces, the powerful,
glitzy to impress the common labourers
an image to instil horror in the disobedient,
create the appearance of life in their parks
away from the gallows of the victims
and the night in irons. Cruelty
in various uniforms goes about its business
and nails the heads of criminals
onto the walls of power. Until one day

19

life crawls over the walls and burns the palace.

Because where there is life there cannot be power.

5

The river is the same river for ever
and is not: its waters constantly stream into the sea.
The fish smell the changes in dissolved chemicals
and begin their journey to the waterfalls
and daringly learn to fly in the air.
The heron wades into the water to gorge himself:
the killing fields are life itself.
The few that escape spawn millions of eggs.

But the rivers have been flowing
as long as there were humans
the Nile, the Congo, the Niger, the Zambezi,
the Limpopo, the Vaal and the Orange,
with ever changing waters ever the same rivers.

Exchange control

nec mora, diversis lapsi de partibus omnes
totaque vertuntur supra caput aequora nostrum.
hactenus acta tibi possum memoranda referre:
hactenus haec memini. nec mens mea cetera
                                           censit.
Without lingering from all sides the streams,
the torrent of the sea floods over my head.
Thus far I can tell you something that is worth
                                     remembering,
thus far I remember. The rest my spirit no longer
                                     felt.
         Publius Ovidius Naso, *Metamorphoses*, Liber 13: 954-957

1

Circulating on the surface of the oceans
warm waters and cold: mist and clouds
rising from the waves, circulating in the air
over land and sea, rain falling and deserts
thirsting for water. Or the freezing ice
on pole caps and mountains raised
by the ever circulating molten core of the earth.
And always the foaming murmur of the waves
as they break against the rocks, the energy
of the winds hurling them into a roar
which blots out my voice: and the rocks remember
the time when suns turned into solid granite,
and gold, long before there was water and a sea.

Plants, too, their seeds wafted by winds and storms
and salty currents, by rivers and animals
move slowly across the land and the waters
inhabiting every nook and cranny,
and in the peaceful sand of the Kalahari
and its motionless solitude one spring morning

the euphorbia closes its night flower, forever.
Kingdoms, families, genera and species,
fighting for a place in the sun or dying out.

And the animals in their amazing variety
populated the earth, always threatened by
extinction,
always flourishing in ever new guises: winged
and heavy-footed, breaking through the thicket
of fern forests and jungles of glossopteris,
catlike and inaudible, every muscle taut
until the final jump which means life or death
on the naked skin of this only planet we have.

2

But humans set up a different circulation,
one, in which the genes were not asked
their opinion: Don't cry. One day we will be able
to say our selves. The market will be closed,
and women will no longer be bartered for cattle,
and beauty will no longer have a price tag.

We have been wrapped in desires,
presents to be unveiled and to cement
families, clans, tribes and nations.
One is not real, and the other an imitation:
the child is the adult, and adults are children.
Whoever is sold, goes through the mirror:
the father becomes husband, the daughter becomes
                                                              mother,
mothering her husband, fucking the father,

suckling the son, and crawling in the dirt of the
                                                              ruler—
mirages, images, heat over the desert, and honour,

22

blood flows endlessly into the sand.

3

Even before the first writing: accountants
in temple precincts with clay tokens
were laying out spreadsheets of gifts
received and tributes due to the God.

Spheres, flat disks, cones, cylinders,
egg shapes and coils, tools, containers
and miniature animals, children's toys,
perverted into a serious game which could end
in death and mutilation for the reluctant tax-payer.

Parabolas, romboids, ovoids, quadrangles
acquired meaning: attached themselves to sounds,
became frozen speech which allowed the king
to enumerate and to rule his subjects,
to build palaces with gleaming blue and golden
tiles.

Bored scribes sat scratching marks into clay
double-entry bookkeeping: and the law
for the subjects never bothered the priests
and the kings above the law. Even then
killing thousands made you a hero; killing one
made you a murderer to be cut to pieces,
to be fed to the vultures outside the gates.

4

Prisoners, their arms tightly bound above the elbow,
were tortured, bearded priests of the Goddess of
                                              Love,
looking on, the tip of the spear turned down:

no pity for the vanquished. Inanna! Inanna!
Dreaming Dumuzi, your lover is doomed.
Your temple was, from the very beginning,
with love for sale and grain against droughts,
a whore house, Inanna! Inanna!
To pay for the glazed mosaics,
to suck up what rulers call surplus,
processions of peasants, sweating in the fields,
delivering wine, oil, goats, sheep and grain
in bevelled rim-bowls and nose-lugged jars
to those who carry their opinion before them
at stomach level. Sealed, stamped and delivered,
the peasants trot home to start their labour again:
I see you wasting before my eyes: you cough,
and the cold creeps up through the bare soil.

5

Five spheres within a sphere,
five grains within a grain,
five eggs on a string: sealed.
Their meaning lost in the darkness of time,
circulating through the dreams of the centuries,
syllables, letters, words, metaphors.

The poem's alphabet derived from IOU's,
is up to its ears in debt to temple scribes
and the orderly circulation of commodities
into the silos of the rich.
I owe you: nobody's without guilt.
The poem circles shame and torture,
crime and punishment:
I am greatly in your debt.
But who is to blame?

6

Circulating on the surface of my brain
tokens in indistinct shapes: mist
rising from the neurones, circulating electricity
through both hemispheres, thoughts falling and
                                        blanks
thirsting for rhymes. Or the freezing depression
in the frontal lobes, and limbs refusing to move
through the ever circulating stream of madness.
And always the murmur of dissatisfaction
as the lines break off without an end, the energy
needed to go on living roaring in my ears
blotting out my voice.

7

Writing is an accountant's skill
from far off temple's in Sumer.
It is the writer's duty to disturb
the symmetry of debit and credit.

A hundred eyes around my head

Centum luminibus cinctum caput Argus habebat
A hundred eyes around his head had Argus
    Publius Ovidius Naso, *Metamorphoses*, Liber 1: 625

1

Words fired into tamed bodies
sitting upright lazily on the couch,
the uninformed become the uniformed:
keep your eyes to yourself!

And this beautiful coastline
stretches to the horizon:
propaganda for the joys of life.
And they show it to you in Technicolor.
And they show you the facts, the facts,
nothing but the facts, and all the facts
(except the ones which they do not want to show
                                you
because they don't want to create
festering wounds of rage!).

2

When the wells dried up,
and the mielies barely pierced the ground
before withering, and the cattle fell
too weak to walk,
but the hut taxes were not reduced,
and the children did not stop
crying for food:
thousands were trekking from the grassless
Transkei

and Zululand
to the big cities:
whose gold was only glitter.
But the mines had more than enough workers
and the shops stood empty.

We would have liked to remain in our villages
but the state had decided otherwise
so one night we were driven into lorries
unfortunately they forgot to feed us
unfortunately none of the lorries was covered
and since they had burned our blankets
we suffered in the sharp night wind.

We were not told where they would take us,
but they unloaded us
among broken, rusty, hanging barbed wire
and dripping water cranes.

If I go mad
a fluttering tongue
hissing like a naked razor
don't lock me up:
permit me to dream
of the silence in the dust
of the sea washing over the sand
of clouds, and
the green jungle in the ear

3

Hunger wrote their epitaph
and the earth does not grow fat
with all the bodies it swallows:

27

Here, where eighteen people
are evicted from a pigsty,
they lived there,
because they could not afford a house,
here, where ten people
are crammed into one poky room,
here, where you are shot, if you say
that your children are starving
and freezing to death.

The supporters of the barbaric death
penalty for treason are shocked,
when the angry crowds impose
the barbaric death penalty on traitors.
Didn't you know that the death penalty
always kills innocents?

4

But when they went down to their graves,
and the sky was grey and depressed
our heroes have been slain
The sky was dark, the wind north-west.

The quarries without dawn,
the wells without water
the caverns without sleep:
We will drown before morning
and no sun is going to wake us.

Petals snow onto the water
covered by mist
the vlei merges with the grey

A dance of sandplovers slows down
the metal blue of the gallinule

disappears behind reeds

Egyptian geese
honk across the silence
of a dream
lost

I weep for Hector Petersen
who was shot by cold-blooded murderers in
uniform
when he was thirteen years old: hero of the
revolution.
I weep for Michael Miranda shot by the police
while playing a children's game in the street.
And I weep for Amanda Fanisi,
suffocated in tear gas
in KTC at the age of six months.
I weep for Noel Letsebe, shot through the heart
at the age of twelve in Alexandra.
And I weep for Stompie Moeketsi Seipei
murdered by a football team.

5

Prime time faces
smooth: hollowing out time
putting their stamp
on thoughtless TV dinners
the president dissolves
in gin and tonic
saturation is reached
before the second sentence
has reached its period

Why are you so shocked,

lamenting in a high-pitched C
with a falsetto voice,
when those, whose children die of hunger,
because the city councillors put up the rent,
kill the children of councillors?

The rich colours
of glowing phosphor
spread and contract
psychedelic boredom
over boere who maak 'n plan
flash news explode
with crumbling buildings
and earthquake shocks
in squinting eyes.

Knives were made to stab,
and fire was made to burn.
Be afraid of the wrath of the people.
It comes in the frenzied mask
of the executioner: with knives,
pangas, and petrol bombs.

But while you wait:
This watered-down orange juice,
this music for gyrating morons,
this commercial disco music for emptyheads,
cosmetic tingling from poisonous herbs,
this tam-di-tam for clammed up oysters.

We all have become fine carriers of coffins
Shouting the pain of the people
in between advertisements for coke
and the big yellow umbrella which covers all
                                        corpses.

One more massacre

1

But what is the meaning of words
and intricate rhythms
when blood seeps through all pages?

What perfection can be wrenched
from the fragments of skulls
and what poem can compete
with the order of weapons?

What beauty is bearable
that has fed on the rotting corpses
of our daily massacres?
And what is the weight of a dream?

And why do we have to speak
after the guns have spoken?

2

This voice in a minor key
speaking after our Sharpevilles and Bishos
cannot compete against the roar of the explosions,
and the dust blown by the rotor blades
of army helicopters
overpowers my breath.

31

But its silence would be a defeat:
for me and for those who died.

Everywhere weapons and order and speech:
against the disorder of feet
walking where they are not allowed to walk,
against the disorder of speech
speaking where it is not allowed to speak.

Blood that has been silenced
needs to speak again in the poem
the poem
which is impossible after the massacre.

3

Because those who kill also talk:
They sell their refurbished tongue
to the highest bidder, their strong-arm tactics
to the most powerful bandit,
their black skin as an alibi
to the white-washed rulers.

At first they agree not to tell
the truth about the crimes of the regime.
But while they walk around in their uniforms,
while they talk in the collaborating councils,
while they preach on hired pulpits,
while they indoctrinate rebellious students,
while they are voted into their separate parliaments
while they learn how to make profits
for the banks in their shops,
they learn: one can not be silent.

You have to justify
what you are doing: step by step

you approve what you denied before.
You do what you denounced before.
You look away from the crimes
they commit: yet you assent
to the bread you receive
for explaining the crimes
of the powerful.

In order to fight apartheid
which oppressed you too
you became a supporter of the regime
to escape the consequences
of apartheid.
In order to fight homelands
you became a homeland leader
or a city councillor
implementing the bantustan policy.
In order to prove your intellectual equality
you became a professor
justifying the subordination
of the oppressed masses.
As you held out your little finger
they took your hand: Now you have become the
handy men
of the system: your hands are bloody.

4

You were wealthy. You were the enemy:
you increased the rent.
You killed hundreds of children,
who died of TB or Kwashiorkor.
You killed hundreds of people
when you called in the police
to protect your home, and the silver coins,
stashed away in a bank account and a shop.

You are the enemy: you are black apartheid.
Your rotting flesh stinks to heaven:
no one can bear your decay any longer.

5

In South Africa
a man is guilty
of his own murder
when he walks unarmed
into a trap of murderous soldiers.

The bully brigadier
is afraid of the bullies
who advance unarmed
against his heavily armoured
line of soldiers
ready to shoot
anyone who crosses the line
behind which
the bully weeps
not because of the slaughter
he has ordered
but because nobody is going to protect him
from unarmed bullies
who will one day soon
string him up
as a common criminal
responsible for countless crimes
against humanity.

6

And the bullet in the back
is for all of us, even if
we don't know it,

even as we still laugh,
and want nothing.

I weep for you Tolani Madikana,
you were not guilty, you were four years old.
It was not your fault that you mother
was elected to the town council.
You didn't know why your mother
stayed on the council, when
the council has done nothing for us.

After the catastrophes

inde genus durum sumus experiensque laborum
et documenta damus, qua simus origine nati.
That is why we are a hard race, experienced in
                                            misery,
thus giving the proof of the origin we came
                                            from
    Publius Ovidius Naso, *Metamorphoses*, Liber 1:
    414-415

1

The colour red: our blood running through black
                                            smoke,
the broken Gods, beautiful but burning
in the conflagration of hate, its blackness consumed
                                            by fire,
it will not help to lie down like the leaves
which have fallen from the trees, in their autumn
                                            colours,
the pool is covered by ashes, its mirror clouded.

Again and again, men and women stand mourning
before their houses burnt down or their children
                                            dead
in famines and droughts, their sons decapitated
or hacked to pieces in senseless wars with
                                            vigilantes,
their daughters raped by a gang of criminals
their cattle driven off by the tax collector.

The earthquake of San Francisco, the tsunamis,
the floods: again and again. In the land between
the two rivers where the first towns were built,

and China's Yellow River and the floods of the river
                                                    Nile,
the droughts which made the Sahara a desert,
the landslides, the ashes of Vesuvius which buried
                                                thousands.

History is a series of fissures which swallow
whole civilisations, because not nature only
but man is destructive, too: fire and explosives,
and the fire ball which rivalled the sun in heat and
                                                    light
which was dropped over Hiroshima by war
                                                criminals
not punished until this day.

Maybe we are made of stones thrown over the back
of this original father and mother, who escaped the
                                                Great Fire
of Zeus and the Great Flood: stonily we watch
the destruction which we create, unable even to
                                                    weep
anymore as the catastrophes multiply electronically.

2

Life always continues after the catastrophes
even if the loss is burned into memory for a long
                                                    time.
The father walks home from the graveyard
where he buried his son to eat as he has eaten every
                                                    day.
The son who was killed in a police cell is not
                                                forgotten,
but the rent is due at the end of the month
and the council threatens to cut off water and
                                                electricity.

The civil war which claimed him continues
with writs from the magistrate attaching the
                                    furniture
which cannot be paid for now, because the son's
                                salary is missing.
The winter rains drip through the holes in the roof
                                    of the shack
and there is no wood anywhere near the township
to make a fire: survival here is a victory,
death is a glorious defeat. Praising the fallen hero
we have to double our efforts to survive the drought
and fight the continuing war against the exploiters
                                and oppressors.

3

The colourful parrots on the bill boards are
drenched
and they shiver in the gale,
the last leafy fingers of this autumn
sink into the wet bank of the cemented river
the flood carries empty bottles, Kentucky Chicken
                                    plastic
cigarette butts, oildrums, dead pigs, beds and
                                    pillows
into the bay towards the drowned cargo ships
where the rats sink to the bottom to form the fossils
of the next geological epoch.

All the cars look as if they are stranded whales
and the jumbo jets plough through metres of brown
                                    water.
There were these joyous coloured lights yesterday
lining the air routes: but they have drowned
with the huts of mud, wood, plastic and beer tins
with the homeless and the tuberculous children

and the unemployed and the women washing
underwear,
where the sandy plains are eternal and soulless,
but one day the rain came down
and the plains were a lake
and they stood in the water and the mud to their
knees.

What else can you do but drink gin to keep you
warm?
It burns like life down your throat and dries your
clothes.

4

The catastrophes play out in large letters
against a the vast backdrop of the African sky
what happens in each family: ruin and violent
death.
The herds are gone, the broken people
in the cobalt haze of the winter morning:
all the fish are stones in the air, ready to kill you
in the black water house under the empty bridges:
but he is not to be found amongst the believers
anymore.
The counting of the single cents in your pocket
does not multiply them so that you can buy bread.

Like the giant figures of the Greek tragedy
ordinary men and women walk to meet their death
to ensure a life which can be lived by humans.

5

Those who dreamed of survival this time
those who believed that they could rebuild

their free market stalls in Disaster Street
and trade with the skeletons of the last war
those who believed that even this catastrophe
could be left behind and a new life could start
on an empty planet purified by fire
were walking through clouds of illusions:

After the CFCs had burned a hole into the ozone
                                        layer,
after the atmosphere filled with carbon dioxide,
after the ice of the Antarctic had melted,
after the last nuclear bomb had been exploded,
the stones started to melt and humans were burned
                                        to ashes
their shadows photographed on granite and cement.

Although we were made of stone
and had eradicated all human feelings
we could not survive the last disaster.

Even the Furies cried

tunc primun lacrimis victarum carmine fama est
Eumenidum maduisse genas.
At that moment, one says, the cheeks of the Furies,
overcome by the song, were wetted with tears
　　Publius Ovidius Naso, *Metamorphoses*, Liber 10: 45-46

1

Creating memories not in severed limbs
and weals across the buttocks, but
with scratches
into stones,
and with colours from plants and minerals,
inscribing magic rituals into clay
baked to last millennia,
drawings and stories onto sandstone
five hundred million years old:

The rain goddess bending down
in black showers towards the parched earth
of Zimbabwe: while the poet dances
his penis half erect and swaying in the wind
among the electric lightning bolts
eight thousand years ago.
The woman on the ground spreading her legs
to receive the rain of fertility:

One of the dreams of God
women married to bulls and swans,
mirrored in writing scribing inscribing
incisions filled with meaning, colour and blackness:
the old heavy trees along the river,
the fury of flowers in unreal colours,

41

the buffalo on its knees, bellowing in anguish,
the stone spear inscribed with the name
of the nameless warrior living forever,
in this Palaeolithic picture poem,
while the cowards splashed their heels with liquid
shit.

2

I know the herbs which grow in the Veld, and
the birds who flit between the branches
and the branches and the trees--
and the flower on the mountain
flowers for me alone.

The forest in the kloofs
whispers secret messages,
intoxication emanates from dark-green leaves,
white powders of ecstasy,
the dragonfly of the rising waters, adrift on the
river,
the mist milling over the mountain ranges,
erica, lilac clouds in the sun, the ribs of a xylophone,
the lament of the elephant drums in the clouds
bewailing the death of a God in the evening sun.

I cut the sheep's throat
and filled the pit with its blood,
Legba must be fed at every sacrifice,
he knows all my clothes and all my whistles
he finds my trail even in water.

The ancestors rose from the waters,
they have come but they walk not, but they walk
not,
they have no eyes but they can see me,

they have a mouth but they cannot converse with
me.
Their presence is overpowering and I speak
the prescribed verses from epics,
magic sentences, thousands of years old,
and they nod to the rhythm of the incantation.

In the clearing I see the pharynx of the night
when the flowers have ended at sunset,
then it is dark and you know what that means,
words from the curve of her lips
and the questions will never end.

3

The unexpected happens forever,
the substance dwindles, the cup is empty,
and what we hope for falters on the horizon.
So what about the stories containing
a high percentage of what we call truth
or alcohol: the last rhapsody of Orpheus,
the scream as he was torn apart by the women.
Human meat rotting among the buttercups and the
clover.
Time for the blackwinged furies to cry.

A moth, a bee, undisturbed by the murder,
a beautiful summer without a conscience,
happy loss of all memory: the past is non-existent
from the earliest virus, continuously separated
from itself to live, to the remnants of the poet
attacked by ants and rats, an illusion, like his play
on the strings of a lyre, a momentary buzz,

food for the scavengers. Fragrance and stink
mingle with the wet scent of the grass.

4

The stones have a memory which lasts longer
than that of the poet: the clay remembers
the words and the figures written by hands
long dead and forgotten. The pages of books
hold the impression of the flourish
which concluded the epic poem
when the hand that moved across the page
has crumbled to chalky dust under a slab
in the monastery's chapel.

5

The sweetness of a voice hiding behind
cursive script in slender volumes remains,
when even her grave has been flattened
by bulldozers excavating a street
through the Israel of her dreams:

I lie at night on your face.
On the pampas of your body
I plant cedar and almond trees.

We don't have much time to write
before some idiot with a gun floors us,
or before we expire in an unmade bed,
unwanted paupers to be interred
by unwilling city fathers.

Franz Marc was bumped off before Verdun
when he was thirty six,
and his dreams were never dreamt to an end:
no colour poured from his downturned mouth
but a piece of jagged glass in his mouth.

The technology of the intellect

Esse viros fama est in Hyperborea Pallene,
qui solant levibus velari corpora plumis,

cum Tritoniacam noviens subiere paludem.
It is said that there are men in the hyperborean
                                        Pallene
who veil their entire body with plumage
after they have dived nine times into the flood
                        of the Tritonian lake
        Publius Ovidius Naso, *Metamorphoses*, Liber 15:
        356-358

1

Gigantic brain stored in alphabetical order:
author, subject, title, theme and topic.
References from any name to any subject
form a spider's web of intelligence
across the sphere wheeling through emptiness.

If this is not God where is he? The totality
of all the lies and all the wisdom buried in print.
A living monument to his death the books
begin to speak as you leave through them
and interrogate the black marks.

But do not crumple the pages of the book:
don't disturb the order of the utterance,
don't break the words by creases and fleshy folds,
don't let the donkey's ears appear on your pages,
don't let the horned one on ram's legs confuse your
                                        meaning.

Beware of the figure at the foot of the letters
supplanting the word,

slippages and thrust faults,
desire which does not speak,
the head lost, the brain drugged by
childhood, paranoia, obsession,
the childish games of the *Autodidasker*,
and letters drifting on water occasionally forming
the word N.I.G.G.E.R or the word J.U.D.E,
the black penis in the triumphant hand
of the *Ystergarde* and the blood,
the visual body of words haunting the poet.

But there are, always, in the geology of the book
pressures, displacements, distortion, disfigurement,
constant revision of all the holy texts,
the grotesque grimace of a god caught in the lust
of the mindless multitude and the temple whores,
and the fundamentalist scream for the blood
of the kaffir and the apostate.

The Egyptian cobra still hisses in every S,
it does not think or judge or calculate,
it is poisonous and brings death:
its shape disavowed and remembered
in a modern type face.

2

This nomadic mobility of the signs
the dance diffused in the body of the reader
reaching across space and time:
feathers growing on my imagination,
wings spread across the waters,
flamingos, and the soft flesh of the plum
with its hard nucleus and the almond, *Amandel*,
the dead in the depth of the dream,
speaking through a strange machine,

emitting smoke and prohibitions,
forbidding you to sift through
the silt covering the mouth of an ancient river
millions of years deep.

As we stand in the desert, an enormous
bare planet floating above the mountains,
we will not call it moon in its dull silvery light,
while scanning the void for inscriptions of hooves
that, too, tell a story reaching back before the
                                                  empires.

It is these tracks that lead to the lost city
and its commercial splendour
where signs are sold for paper gold,
and the tin can money ejaculates from machines.

But the tracks are an escape route
if you go in the other direction
where nothing has been lost
except the silence of the written word
in the sand, extinguished by every wind.

Move, my camel, move: we will find the burning
                                                  bush
in the last volume hidden away in the dusty corner,
where nobody has been for years.
This is where the miracle will happen,
where the young woman meets the god
who traverses the length of the years
and sees everything that there is to see on earth
and who feeds his horses the food of the gods.

And he will say -- in the book -- I love you.
Truly. You must trust me.

Only here, amongst the letters, and hidden
amongst it the S, the god is truly golden.

3

This thing is secret. Go now! Leave!
Nobody should plant secret microphones
when the god speaks to his beloved.
Nobody should witness the holy terror of the
                                        woman
who finally sees the god in his nakedness
carrying his rigid sex before him.

But jealousy always has a telescope
that distorts the ecstasy into tears,
jealousy always creates another,
who watches and listens and tells.

The father, the brute, buries love
and covers it with sterile sand,
six feet underground, still alive,
still breathing, entreating the brute,
betraying the god. But she is planted,
the tree of incense, the bloody innocent body
which gods demand, always, as an offering
for their shiny love: to rise to the heavens
as the wonderful stench of love
to amuse the eternally cruel gods.

4

Phantasm is the rhythm of a living voice
pulsing in everything that lives,
calling out over the desert: chanting
the story of love and murder: the poet's tongue.
And the fairy tale of resurrection as a tree.

It is an order which distributes the bones of the
                                        father
in another way than the holy books:
they swing like the penis of the advancing rapist
from a bitter tree in the breeze.

He will put her into a hole.
He will put his into her hole.
His bones rattling
like the clapper of a maddened bell
across the cemetery demanding
the resurrection of order.

5

It is always the son who gets nailed to the tree.
And three days later he is resurrected
to become a father like all fathers before:
rising to the heaven to sit on the right hand side
of the father, who speaks and speaks and speaks.

The daughters are buried so that should not know.
So that they should not speak the unspeakable.
The dream that cannot be made to speak.

The vast library spanning the globe
is silent: never
may any word say what happened in that hole
where the incense tree died and then grew.

6

All along the lines and lines of books
there are hidden conversations,
oscillating between sameness and nearness,

49

formal repetitions, the trauma recurs
from Gilgamesh to The Palisades, Los Angeles.

The wisdom does not get wiser,
the transgressions multiply,
metaphors proliferate and transport
meanings across the globe,
the constraints are not inscribed in language,
the marriage of words not authorised,
the confusion is not disentangled.

If you approach too close
it is too late: you are part of the scene,
required to play your part: god or maiden.
In the converging headlights of police trucks
the tragedy is re-enacted as bloody farce:
bodies, cut like butcher's carcasses
in the boot of a car, a motionless face, a rifle.

The story continues: echoing
in the Fish River Canyon and the Maluti Mountains,
the goddess is burned as a witch,
the trees are scarred by the lightning
of an indigenous Zeus,
the spark ignited by the promiscuity of two words:

When Legba found his wife deflowered by Fa,
she said: Your penis is not enough for me.
So Legba gorged himself and sang before all the people:
Gudufu, the path of my destiny is large, large, large
like my large penis. O Gudufu, you are large.

But he did not hear the laughter of the gods:
because it is not a question of size
but the lure of the gold in the eyes
and the words on the tongue.

Survivors

The poor interred corpses
of the Cape Flats

In the evenings, when the South Easter abates
in the plastic sheets of the squatter huts
on the Cape Flats the poor interred corpses
sink deeper into wet sand of the vleis.

Later at night there is a rain which falls noisily
onto the corrugated iron and all the blood
is washed away. The last drops fall cautiously
like the promise of futures into the sand.

When the wind is still and the rain
is a mere memory of drops from Port Jackson leaves
the darkness swims into the hearts of the sleepers
and makes them restless with undefined fear.

They hold their breath for minutes of silence
and know that something new is about to happen,
something good, something which was an absence
in their lives for hundreds of years.

8 June 1994

Lines in a graveyard

That was the bad old time
when he lived: the time
when children died of
incurable emptiness of the stomach
and the country
had an elegant medical term for that.

That was the bad old time,
here represented in numbers which designate
the year of birth and the year of death,
now engraved on the gravestones
which have survived into our time,
and the stones begin to speak
about that disease which made children die.

8 June 1994

The Cape weather and the five year plan

Like old men, the clouds piss
when they can no longer hold their water,
and the last pied crow
shakes its feathers in disgust
in the grille of tangled branches.

Leafless oaks hold their upturned roots
into a gale of leaden laughter
erupting from forgotten graves
clearing the skies to an icy blue
and yesterday's news is driven against the wire
                                        mesh
of our sieve-like memory: which Marx did you
                                        mean?

With chattering teeth the cracked skulls
caught in the grating of the sewerage system
repeat the slogans shouted with such confidence
seven long years ago at their grave side.
A solitary woman woven in the trellis of pain
her wrists broken, but alive, not like a runner
who has reached her goal, but not like a corpse
                                        either,
simply breathing in this wonderful new disorder
and creative chaos breeding under the sun
which begins to melt the snow on the mountains.

Images which speed across the spherical
splintered mirror inside my skull
in retrograde circles of dulled pain
while we spend our time,

skin, bones, meat on some brilliant white sand
a short span of time in an eternity
a life and two cv's on this warm winter's day
the sun above and the darkness below.

28 July 1994

Mayibuye Centre

Some men and some women
stepped into the flash light
once
for one hundredth of a second
and lived in darkness for the rest of their lives.

Therefore we know
how they looked
those
who lived in the shadows
in one hundredth of a second
of the two billion five hundred million seconds
which made up their life.

8 June 1994

On the assassination of Chris Hani
10th April 1993

1
as we are
slowly
sucked in by the slime
and the mud
of a dying regime

our heroes fall
in their drive ways
executed by the mad men
we educated in the past
in the art of shooting
and torturing

thus we drown
with grim determination
while our houses burn
to ashes
our children bleed to death
and our books disintegrate
silenced by the crack of guns

2
you were frightened
not of their guns
but of the poverty
crippling women
and children and men

you ended in a pool of blood
because

you did not love
the misery
and the hunger
and the mass-produced murder
which were the gross
national product
of this our state

3
in the hour of snakes
and confused electronic dreams
when we lost courage
you came
bleeding
into the evening room
a chimera of electrons
and you talked about peace
as if you were still alive

and you
still visible still preaching
reconciliation
were already
beyond reconciliation
and married to the shadow
and to the earth
which you liberated

4
the milky dawn
re-echoes with the shouts
of crowds drunk
on the slogans of yester-year
and castle lager beer

married
to the blue metal of their guns

as if we walk through hell
its endless expanses
littered with the bloodless spirits
of those who were murdered
by the insanity
of our greed
determined not to share
anything
we stare with lidless eyes
across burning corpses
into our uncertain future

We are our enemies

whirling
stones across the space
between
enemy and enemy

the night is full of gleaming metal
as malnourished youngsters
attack starving greybeards

the exploited fight those
who are unable to find work
the hostel-dwellers
shoot out of their barred windows
hitting dwellers in shacks

every stone is hurled back
every bullet returned
blood washed in blood
fire extinguished by fire

clutching a gun
like everybody else
there is no target
but the will to survive
turning in screaming circles

abandoned
like the first dead
in this orgy
which has lasted for years
I am a prey to the sky
which is filled with

guns on wings

chained
to my desire
I live
my own life
fragile between the battle fronts
in the darkest shadows
drifting in this madness typhoon
racing towards death

my own
enemy

Colour bars in front of our eyeballs

like prisoners walled in
colour bars in front of our eyeballs
in a fever of expectations
we listen to everyday sounds
and the threat underneath them

as we sit and talk about peace
in the midst of our words
the sudden wild scream
hundreds of huts catch fire
and sharpened spears
find their way to the beating heart
of our nation
openings which go down
into the earth like empty wells
echoing uncertainties

the birds fall and die
the ivy whispers unconfirmed rumours
and red leaves tumble
from the wall
into the black of our eyes

As a child I could fly

as a child I could fly
I just stretched out my arms
and the storm lifted me
into the clouds

gliding like a buzzard
I was dreaming
in my eyes
the curve of the river

and the forest
on the belly of the mountain
down to the quarry
with its ammonites

grown in a tropical sea
millions of years ago

As long as the dreamer dreams

without a sound
the water was rising
between the shacks
beds began to circle
children disappeared
under the brown flood
cars and buses drowned
and the great terrifying love
the passions of murderers
and of suicides drowned
in the slowly rising waters

the airport drowned
and the loudspeakers
announced endless delays
all incoming flights were cancelled
while the giant Boeings
swam like whales
to the ocean: to give birth

helicopters
fell from the sky like hailstones
churning up the flood
before they sank
into the mud

a lonely child
paddled his bathtub
down to the harbour
and set off across
the Atlantic Ocean
on a journey of discovery

From the underground

this country
has been packaged
behind the glass
of countless tv screens

the media quote
ever the same soundbites
and market
ever the same images

the attention span
of the average non-reader
is 30 seconds
and diminishing

this country
doesn't desire
words which come
from the underground

fear me
love me
now that nobody is thirsty
and the books are dusty

like dynamite
in a forgotten cellar

We take the time that is given

love, we do not love, as their fairy tales
prescribe: we take the time that is given
and transform it into fireworks
of short-lived words exploding
and dropping from the sky
white stones deep into the well

Grandmothersalesmen

I always knew that I was a hopeless case:
salvation was not for me
my bank-balance shows it
even my poems grow mouldy
in the endless rain
and the halo in my kitchen cupboard
needs some Brasso polish

but I don't trust them: these grandmother-
salesmen, they beat truth to a pulp
on their ornate pulpits, while
shivering stars, frozen blue in this night
swim through the late-revolutionary smoke
rising from the altars of these crazed priests
of the eternal status quo

they rape my sister language with
their violinated prayers
and light up the sky with rotating crosses
gold on blue
love poems to a crucified liar
while they fill in
insurance policies on vellum payable on
the day after the end of the world

I only manage a confused shout
in four voices: shit! but forcefully
before I am dragged before the altar
and my throat is slit for the sixteenth time
by these pinstriped murderers
in the name of whatever volk or people

Statement to the press

O.K.
that's it then
you don't want to listen
and I have no more desire
to convince you of anything

If you insist that the sky is red
and that the earth is about to explode
or that Jesus is coming tomorrow
I will not contradict you:
because what use are contradictions
in a single paragraph
hidden away among the society photos
and the astrology column

No more courting,
I have outgrown this mode
of speaking
no more screams for help
and no more pleas for understanding

Instead a silence
as impenetrable as a rock
lasting longer than any poems
on fragile paper
in any book
collecting dust
in an unused library

Dr Gottfried Benn, he dead, but the baboon has a colourful arse

Dogs and jackals have their song,
the baboon has a colourful arse,
biology and rugby,
or the national flag,
and thousands shouting hoarsely
their belonging to something,
and maybe some prefer
arpeggios and choral music
and the paintings of Watteau.

I prefer mind music
inaudible: fugitive
and no respite
abrupt
transitions
foreshortened.

I do not keep my metaphors
clean and uncontaminated,
but I do have problems
        with my unconscious,
aggression, sex and the Oedipus.

I mourn the decline of the English language
as much as any of my neighbours,
but you can't have an empire
of people who all speak like your uncle
in Somersetshire. And a bit of miscegenation
can only do the tired old language good.

I do not norm the gases

which leave my various body orifices,
and when I piss, my penis drips.

Painted in the blood of red berries
I eat poisonous mushrooms
and smoke pot.
I reach my home dreaming
of a garden in the mountains
overlooking the silver mirror
of an irreal Table Bay.

Mirrors are no defence against nausea

Every morning
I switch on my electric razor
to trim my beard
into respectable proportions.

The face in the mirror
has grown stranger
over the years
and I have refused it permission
to use my name.

I tried very hard not to see
what happened behind the mirror.
Nobody likes to be reminded
of the shortness of life.
But the flaking mercury
made the mirror a window
into the chasm.

I have been born

There is a rumour
that I have been born.
There is little that I can say
about this rumour.

As far as I can remember
I was not present at the event
and I hate gossip

There is even a document
which states that I was born
on such and such a day
in a town in Eastern Europe
but that document
is probably a falsification
even if it looks tattered and much used
an attempt by a little town
dependent on the tourist trade
to add another poet
to its hot water springs
and the famous pair Goethe
and Ludwig van Beethoven
who used to spend their vacation
steaming
in the Schlangenbad
and promenading in the park

On the other hand
the story that I spent five years
in Catholic Bavaria
seem to be not without any foundation
although I do not want to rely

73

on my memory alone
and the fact that I remember
a cow that attempted to gore me
one late summer
means nothing really
as such authentic memories
are often a cover for much more painful
memories: love and delusions of grandeur

I am slightly more certain
about the Black Forest
although I certainly was not born there
and whether I ever met Heidegger
is the subject of an anecdote
which cannot be verified
since Heidegger has died in the meantime

I can say with some certainty
that I was not born in Hluhluwe
although the call of the bush shrike
meanders through some of my poems
and Johburg was no more than a station
than Cape Town
in the constantly shifting geography
of my life

The name Inkululeko is a late legendary
addition to the confused biography
of a rootless cosmopolitan intellectual
who was at home nowhere
except in libraries and on the waves
of the eternal ocean
that links the continents
of this earth

Another repetitive corpse on our screens

Who then is safe
in this land of the gangsters
on government pay,
gangsters who murdered Goniwe
and now protect us
against murderers?

Our future is held hostage
by horse-riding psychopaths
in brown shirts
and an unspeakable triple seven,
gigantic dwarfs who play at war
but with real guns.

Men fall from moving trains
every day
and the train drivers
duck to avoid the little holes
made in their windscreen
by anonymous bullets

But these are men,
they have wives children mothers fathers uncles,
these are real men
not some Hollywood hero
who gets up after he has been shot
and wipes the blood off his mouth
and is quite realistically alive.

They really lie in a pool of blood
their one leg twisted
in an anatomically absurd position

one half of their face missing
and they are really dead
and this is not some gangster movie
but the eight o'clock news.

It makes little difference
to them
whether they were killed
in a taxi war or an Inkatha hostel
or an ANC squatter camp.
These things are of little import
when you are dead.

Your eyes

Of all that is alive and moves
on this spacious earth
I love most your eyes
which mirror this world lovingly.

8 June 1994

I have forgotten who I am

The temptation to forget this time in which I live,
and to hand over my body parts to be redistributed
to the clouds and the sea and the mountain.

My heart feels nothing as the water washes over my
                                                    belly,
the scales are balanced, the seconds equally spaced,
the mellow warmth of a late day in August,
bergwind warm for a Cape winter's day.

Meaning is a pattern of Namaqualand daisies
red, yellow and black covering the sandy soil.
When the grass begins to grow between the cobbles
the time has come: eternal green smothers
the transitory granite.

Glossary:

Urgestein (German) : Granite. Goethe wrote an essay on the earliest rocks found in Germany.

Ding an sich (German): The thing as such. Immanuel Kant maintained that the things as they are, are not accessible to our knowledge, only the phenomena, the appearances are.

Autodidasker: actually: *Autodidakt*, a self-taught person, quoted by Sigmund Freud as an example of paranoid language formation.

Nigger, Jude (German): Negro, Jew

Ystergarde (Afrikaans): paramilitary formation of the rightwing *Afrikaner Weerstandsbeweging*

Legba, Fa, Gudufu : characters in Nigerian mythology

Dr. Gottfried Benn, 1886-1956, famous German poet.